Persephone
(2021 Orphic Journal I)

Kit Ludlow

ISBN: 9798728016366

Ce-way Ne

Mora Me

Mo Chlann

WHY SONNETS?

Most of the poems here are sonnets. Sonnets as they are defined here: fourteen lines, one hundred forty syllables, structured in four three lined stanzas and an ending couplet. End lined rhyme with a centered stanza echoed rhyme. (ABA CBC DED FEF GG).

Conventional, yes. Formal, yes. Mathematical, yes. Out of this time, yes. Timeless, yes.

Speaking only for myself. Sonnets are the greatest poetic form. The short-structured form allows for quick, essay-like lyrical style that captures a moment. They are NOT overwrought or workshop lines that clothes the rawness of poetry and recast it as a model of beauty- a freak of nature. I would rather write one hundred sonnets and flash lightning like an insect than rewrite a single sonnet into a synthetic diamond and suppressing the rest. I favor a democracy in creativity and find no gem greater than the rest (if they are natural).

The poems within are literally from a journal, a lineal sequence of the conscious and unintentional subconscious (the subconscious can be drawn up from the conscious at times regardless what any philosopher or psychologist will say otherwise). Some of the lyrical portions of Orpheus are included. The narrative is not. How many journals will there be? How long will I keep up with it? I don't know. There are two now (Persephone and Hades). They might reflect a seasonal structure and theme. For right now, they do.

03/24/2021

Prologue:

True Love, search not in these unholy sonnets,

Lines, a requiem for the wreck we made.

There are none. They are fashioned gems like onyx.

Hard to penetrate- they absorb the light-

Shift the energies- find shadow from shade-

And cleanse the mind ticking toward midnight.

I feared the rhythm - tick- that breath of air.

Time has always been the present, my curse,

Because I can exist with everywhere.

In that knowledge, fate has told me I must

Erase the line between poet and verse

Before paper becomes yellowed and dust.

So here are my shanties, my words of play,

Disoriented by shipwrecks of each day.

02/1/2021

I.

I stopped for Death but Death wouldn't stop for me.

Instead, she blew a kiss, whispered "someday"

And walked on by- sex in the century-.

The day I tried to kill, I had to live.

The Pain-I-felt, no poetry could say,

Found no pleasure in the all I could give.

I gave Death the name, Beauty, and I wept.

The Shame-I-was deserved not HER sweet praise;

What I treasured reflected me unkempt.

In sorrow, I made the public a masque;

And I played many parts to be like them.

Fool them, did I? Dulled the senses and fact.

The fact etched into my whole being:

I had to live for her death to want me.

II.

And I wanted Death but. . . Hers in my arms?

No, I didn't. I wanted her scent on me-

"Others would think of me. Leave her unharmed."

That's what I thought. I wanted just her touch,

The feeling of warmth in sheets, the being

Of suspended in time- a soulful much.

Never had the desire to ravage her-

Thought no one had that desire: - Misery! -

Or possess her to keep things as they were.

I wanted a belonging- a mother's love-

That intense magnet-pull against feeling-

The falling before a reach from above.

That above now tells me in rhyme, ? in meme ?:

To keep on living until death wants me.

III.

And what is living? An inhale of breath.

A Shakespearean actor, honey lines,

And a constant lust-flirtation with Death.

That is a tragedy that had its stage.

What about the failure? The silent cries-

The beaten, endowed with sorrowful rage.

A real time that can't be kept from a page?

Or a story? Make it short. Gives more time.

Time. Time. Broken clock. Time cannot be caged.

And what about theses verses made private?

A male Dickinson? A joke, if anything.

Words of Greatness cannot be kept quiet.

And does greatness come in sonnets' couplets?

Living a life, full of sex and drug sweats?

IV.

Or just being alive, waiting for death.
Is that what life is? A belief in joy-
A nurse-joy that numbs the diminishing breath.

Or is it? The attempt to fix a fate-
An unagreeable one- no one enjoys-
That's a chorus- a cancer that I hate.

Truth is: I am embarrassed to live.
'Cause I want Death and I am her? That ploy?
Here should stand a line I wish I could give.

I'll try to purge what I am- stand naked;
Allow this to be my voice- not a Howl,
An echo in Dante's woods or a note vacant.

These words are not mine. I didn't invent them,
But I'll use them to live a life condemned.

V.

A life condemned to find meaning in sounds,
Not pulsing from this heart- not from nature-
But from a democracy of verbs and nouns. -

That is what I have? Prometheus fire,
Unbound, while I endure the Gods' torture?
What will my children know of desire?

The desire to burn- a witchcraft passion
To perform the spells that inspires the dead
To draw in breath, echo out in action. . .

Or to rearrange the matter of things-
Morph what I see to shine a pale moonlight
On the shipwrecked coasts of Death's many flings.

And what of Death? Her history of lovers?
I want to be one bound by her covers.

VI.

Birth and death- the covers of every book-

The engraved dates upon many gravestones-

Haunts me because of what's within. The look!

The look of blank pages. Lessons unlearned.

Adventures never made. The skin and bones-

The repose in a coffin. . . Unconcerned.

I want Death, not a sleep away from life.

No one ask to be born- that is well-known;

A truth that reads as cliché, a dull knife.

Agree? Then it is within my own right

To ask for Death, her lips pressed against mine,

The uneven breaths, gasp and grasps in the night.

What is written here will perplexed many.

Some even fear her- Death-Persephone.

VII.

Persephone- I have named my own death.
I need no pomegranate seeds to ingest.
No trick to stay, run away, be of breath.

I need no crown. No underworld to rule.
Only your presence- I truly confess -
Be with me, a love of two spheres, dual.

And I do not expect an answer yet.
My soul is shedding this prison of flesh;
The disgusting mask of pain and forget.

Do not think these verses as suicidal.
Suicides, masters of their own demise,
Desire rest, not a lover that's bridal.

Wait for me to prove myself above all:
The bards of voice and makars' flyting-brawl.

VIII.

Sleeping mountains can become volcanos
The smoldering- a passion to be felt,
Held far too long must become of great flows.

Destruction lies in the wake. All varied,
But remembered by those who did not melt.
Ash falling like snow. Villages buried.

The ordinary persevered to be viewed,
Centuries later as frozen in time,
A lesson that humans aren't me and you.

We are the stills- towering in the sky-
Holding back the eruptions of our souls
That changes landscapes, that defy the why.

We do what we do. That is our nature.
Science can define. We are the creator.

IX.

My lips sip liber's tea of liberty-

And I am so drunk that I sing of thee-

Death, who finds me too alive, too in need.

Me? A poor man stealing bits of knowledge,

Those born rich find common in the Ivy.

Desire has made my own mind a college.

Even when I am impaired, I can write-

Write lines that make readers feel destiny-

That they were destined to understand this rite.

Call it the arrogance of skill. - I do!

No eyes have brought witness; no lips have kissed

These words with sound. And, yes, this will come true:

All I have written; all I have compose:

Will find itself marked read by my life's close.

01/23/2021

X.

Critics would have me edit out the phrases;
Odes to clichés- the common expressions,
Therefore, become original by their praises.

Too often I have disfigured one grace
To beautify another passion;
And, in so, made an unnatural face;

One that cannot look in a mirror
Or in the eyes of creature-companion
Without shrieking at the horror, terror. . .

The terror of living as a golem.
Alive, they're alive. Totally fashioned
By their creator to walk among them.

You cannot be immortal and alive;
Embrace the immemorial or a lie.

01/24/2021

XI.

You live many days- you only die once.

Lay me high upon a mountain- alone.

I don't care if those below call me "dunce".

There I will live, my lungs full of icy breath-

My skin bitten. My limbs heavy as stone. . .

All until my suffering pleases Death.

Let the vultures scatter my bones about,

Feel my flesh in their guts, nourishing them,

So, they can take flight, fertilize a sprout-

The sprouts of nature that feeds all the shoals.

Perhaps others will find along the stems

A recluse of body, not of the soul.

Let these poems be fragments of myself,

Spread to earth's corners not just on its shelf.

XII.

Call it blasphemy. I'm not one to trust

A heaven's bargain in the flames of hell

And to forgo one desire to please lust.

Of what I speak- let the words themselves tell,

While I mutter to myself- a play's fool,

A Hamlet, who knows madness in him dwells.

I rhyme and rhyme. Wind, so wintry, so cruel,

Carry my echoes out as I descend

The spirals of torment, in which I rule.

I could stop. . . But if I would, I will lose

These soliloquies, this stage of sin,

And weep angel-tears, let music seduce.

True faith requires an inferno of pain,

Smoldering, searing away what is shame.

01/25/2021

XIII.

Forever is another name for Death-
Skeletons never rise from their repose,
Shake off the worms and grow lungs full of breath.

Rivers, flow shallow, some even go dry,
Always expecting rain or the melting snow
To replenish what's been lost over time.

Drought can end that bloodline, though veins persist
And new waterways will settle in place,
Preserving that a cycle will exist.

That course may seem like an eternity,
Until the sun consumed by its own pace
Obliviates earth from a reality.

These tears too shall vanish under a heat-
Relax it's just a plague we'll defeat.

XIV.

You say I have hidden myself in shame.

I'll unclothed veiled thoughts for you to view,

To know what is hammering in this brain.

A pain: the unwrapping of the present:

You wish to spend no moments, old or new,

Not spaces of time- actual events....

And in the preferred state lives no hatred,

Yet no care for the future once pursued

And the making that finds yourself naked.

What are vows but mu•ti•lated sounds of air,

In which two muted latent change of moods,

Believing passion wouldn't have this affair.

No one should have doubted my love for you;

You were the uncertain, not false or true.

01/26/2021

XV.

A firefly among the stars, short and dull.
To have a universe within oneself
And illuminate out thoughts from the skull.

That's how I glow, even when I'm contain,
Trapped in a bell jar on a bedroom shelf,
A dash- a comfort to those that feel pain:

The pain of silence on a restless night.
The night is full of wonder-wanderings
What should I not fly in them, burst with light?

Because life is brief? The moon hangs above.
Its shine reflected, not a self-burning.
Seasons pass, clouds gather- it casts its love.

Brilliance is not measured by time or show.
It is a fluorescent of what you know.

XVI.

The Quarantine- the purgatory- the year:
A raven-haired mistress of the bell
Speak an unspoken message you can hear:

The invisible hand twirling your hair,
The depression-priest of heaven AND hell,
The unlit poet-candle, the ensnare,

Sage not. Raki it. Distill the summon.
Sip the ayahuasca, inhale the weed,
Until you can find truth in the sermon.

Welcome the spirit, good or bad in faith,
Into the collective humanity,
The Spiritus Mundi, congress of wraith.

The limbo of this existence echoes
Over the centuries, bones in meadows.

01/27/2021

XVII.

Bones in the meadows, creatures of the marsh,

Long since drowned, lost in the depths of time,

Resemble your form, be it full or harsh.

I know my place among you all- the height,

Not a star to guide you toward Christ's crime-

Faulting wrongs in the name of what is right.

I have no apostles. - Only sacred texts,

Words so secret that they could be on stone

And centuries later unearthed to sects-

The cults that seek a truth in poetry.

I am poet, not a poem alone-

That is my high-place: on the balcony.

From stone to scroll to paper to ink-light,

The words of a poet survive the blight.

XVIII: GME

The vultures, hovering, earning flight miles,
And the dung beetles, gathered in mass,
Scavenging what they can from the piles.

A fable for those feasting just for sport-
The beetles, once seen noble in the past,
Band together, resurrect life made short.

The bet made long. The vultures grow hungry;
They are predators for the weak and last,
And see the scheme head toward bankruptcy.

Vultures, voices raspy, call for a beast
To kill the preserved, trample out the nest
And they will take shares in the after-feast.

In the end, the sky lords over the scene
And beetles scatter, "rules for me, not thee".

XIX:

Rock-a-bye baby in the daddy's arms.

If he drops you, you will come to great harm.

And if he drops you, you'll fall on your head.

And the doctor will come by and say . . .

Baby is brain-dead.

Rock-a-bye baby, dolled eyes rolled back.

If he shelfs you, you will never have cracks.

And if he shelfs you, you'll gather some dust.

And the collector will come to say. . .

Baby is a must.

Rock-a-bye baby in the cradle rots.

If he traps you, you will stay as he thought.

And if he traps you, you'll never be free

And the taxidermist will display. . .

Baby is beauty.

Rock-a-by baby, listen to this song.

I hold you, sing this to you, right or wrong.

XX.

This heart's pulse: a tick from the doomsday clock-
A hundred seconds left until midnight-
A full moon- crystals to absorb and block.

Creak from ceiling fan- body slips from soul.
Smoke steps to pool- mediation in flight.
What's not from within, isn't yours to control.

One cannot journey without leaving home-
The home that is childhood. That voice is loud.
What of us that are orphans, those alone?

Resist the tunnel, if not sure of step.
Light travels fast. You may find all fog-shroud
And lose oneself caught in fate's sticky web.

Crazy wisdom from shaman of madness
Teach me what is the matter of darkness.

01/28/2021

XXI.

O, soul of fire trapped in a hell of ice,
Burn so bright to melt away the avowal:
Mortals must be punished in cells of vice.

The prettiest songs are those sung so nice
That the lyrics are syllable-sounds of vowels.
I wish I had the voice of paradise.

What I can do is put words into rhyme-
Craft lines so antique that meaning is dowels.
What I am is ancient, lost in a mine.

Free me from the fleshy prison of aches,
The devils' pitchfork stabs in my bowels,
And I will shine through what the world mistakes.

Despite what is believed and what's been told:
True diamonds are not form from lumps of coal.

XXII.

A fable, written and then forgotten:

An orphan, abandoned in a coal mine,

Seek a home in a town of greed and sin.

He'll trade what he has- what he can carry:

Tattered clothes, a fist of coal and his mind.

All declined. No riches in that quarry.

Gamblers try to recruit him as a peek,

Thieves try to teach him to pickpocket dimes,

And brothels promise to make him unique.

All he has to do is free up his hand.

He refuses- disappears for some time.

He returns as a savior to that land.

Few realized the pressure placed on that soul;

The diamond hand was once a fist of coal.

XXIII.

Mediation- a funeral of mind-
No mourner-cry to disturb the quiet,
Only a plunging deep into sublime.

There I can see you- lips red from a wine
And eyes, knowing the silence of riot.
You say nothing. Others come near to dine.

Worms squirm, the flies buzz above where I lie.
You tip your glass. Thoughts turns to your diet.
In them, whispers on the science of a vine:

Those harvest in youth are a sweet missing.
Those aged with dust taste bitter and defiant.

And I am soon thrust back into living.

And Death, you will want me still on your tongue
But it is you who will lie in my song.

XXIV.

And lie you will in truth or a repose.

I refuse to keep you at a distance

Or hidden- a mistress for me to pose.

For some, you're a Siren upon the crags. -

A trick to pull oneself from existence

Or to obtain pleasure between your lags.

I am not shipwrecked, near-drowned on your beach.

I am the nobody, tied to the mast

And the bard that can sing over your reach.

I don't need you to be or not to be.

That's not vanity- you know my past.

No you. No me. No you and me. Just we.

We know the seasons- the truth of the all.

You are the muse. I am your Kit, the call.

XXV.

Fame is a forbidden fruit to favor,

Even for those not barred from the Garden.

Once consumed by it, you are the flavor.

Yes, wisdom does come from being the tree,

Rooting yourself in the soil of certain,

But to be cultivated? No, not me.

I'll spend my days, away from the well-known,

The serpent hiss of immortality,

A reality that's not mine to own.

The dawn of an eclipse- a black hole sun.

Clouds: incomplete view of totality.

Rose-petals close. - Cicadas' songs undone.

This is what I feel: madness in nature,

Not harmonies of routine and nurture.

02/01/2021

XXVI.

In this: a constant state of expressing,
You read it as madness. I see a storm
And a type-rope act that keeps you guessing.

I feel cold when a spotlight is on me:
Some feel the heat and sweat. Others the warm.
I stand naked as an obscenity.

On stage, you can be the east and the sun.
That's not me! I can survive in darkness.
In a sideshow, advertised to be fun?

Circus of freaks, yes. I can cast that scene.
Be it a club foot, blindness or madness,
Poets master a true disability.

Mine? A silt-tongue. A slow thought. A deep need
To hear my words in the mouths of many.

XXVII.

Emily's I and Milton's light. Those are tropes?
The sex of passion. The gender-constraints.
The neurotics that search in poems hope.

The chains bind us down. Birds pick at our flesh-
And we still bring fire to those in the faints,
The playthings of the god- children of ash.

We pick at our wounds because they are there,
Already being exposed and tortured.
Often our verse exists as a prayer.

What will pain me until I'm fully dead?
Without a shutter, slur or murdered word,
I can't speak like the voice inside my head

Please know what is written is my true voice;
It hasn't been fashioned in this style by choice.

XVIII.

Life is not renewed by anger: thunder;

Growth comes from tears that waters the soil.

Even when flooded, all is not sundered.

Flowers will sprout from the turf- weed or not-

And repopulate the garden, once spoil,

Proving that not all has to come to naught.

Those of us, blessed with green thumbs, can manage;

Others pay for a conservatory,

And the dutiful can mend the damaged.

We have never been banished from Eden;

We have been told so in many stories.

Feel your heart. - That paradise lies within.

We are each other's tender - not keeper-

No other fact can pierce so much deeper.

02/02/2021

XIX.

I have never seen a ghost. - Only rooms,

Where hearts beat a rhythm like a dancer

In the slow unraveling of a doom.

Lips tremble to pronounce what's on their mind.

So many questions- there must be answers.

The sadness in their eyes when there's no why.

To be so helpless, held hostage by time.

That is the true horror of these cancers-

Even when we transplant them to a prime.

Torn by the torment of so many lives,

Who can continue as a necromancer

When all that survive is living with lies?

I know what I have to do, be stillness,

A comfort light in the gathered darkness.

XXX.

To know war without taking up the fight.
That's a trauma that's hard to justify-
You do it to survive, to have a life.

Warm bright sunlight on a harsh winter day. -
The heat- if you are sheltered- can revive,
But outside, you are chilled- the clouds are gray-

Tears are so frozen that they can't be cried.
You tend to the wounded and those who'll die-
No secret healing. You'll try and have tried.

Applause comes from those you resurrected. -
It is the silence - that is deafening-
From dead never risen- the neglected.

How do you explain to those in the grave
The feeling: you murder what you can't save?

02/03/2021

XXXI.

True beauty, like time, cannot be altered.
The yesterdays and nows are forever
Even if preserved or unsheltered.

Styles change like paint on Grecian marble.
Statues lose limbs- purpose not remembered-
Centuries later, we stop and marvel.

Art is souvenirs of a soul's journey-
A ghost tale- a year without summer-
A compass to a place in history.

And what is true? Denial and doubt thrives.
Alternative frictions- the mad fever-
All are drawn to a nature that survives.

The emotion, the chemical in me:
Love for you- that is the truth of beauty.

XXXII.

These leaves of grass- these ink-tears in your hands

Binds the failures along with the success.

Pluck from them what you want, what you demand.

The trouble of a troubadour: - the deaf,

Haunts the purpose of every letter pressed,

Not the notes that do falter off the clef.

When those hear snicker, there comes loneliness.

Doubt can plague the mind as an illness

Suppressing verse to tings of idleness.

The anxiety that follows the pain-

A sky curtained by a grey of stillness-

A cloister bell- a pulse within these veins.

Long I have traveled, bitten by a frost,

To discover I had never been lost.

02/06/2021

XXXIII.

Let a future stranger discover me
Like a single red rose plucked from a bush
And pressed inside a book of obscurity.

Perhaps they will question the purpose,
The significance- a Kingdom of Kush
Nearly eradicated from the surface.

A city of necropolises stands,
Overlooked by the breathing centuries
And half-withered among the shifting sands.

There you will find artifacts of a life,
Free from past prejudices and miseries
That brought remembrance to blight, a strife.

Deconstruct these words like bricks, build a wall-
But the origins will remain in the sprawl.

XXXIV.

Sink or swim- the trial of the accused.

I have remained afloat throughout these years;

A trick of power few have ever used.

The town folks, who feared me, returned home safe-

Forgetting why I was thrown from the pier

Or thinking water claimed me as a waif.

And what was my crime? The dull-tongue, slow speech?

The recall- a madness of remembrance?

Or the lack of belief in what they preached?

I couldn't and would never blend with the crowd.

My spirit is tuned to a resonance,

Conjurers have spelled out in verbs and nouns.

I'm no lady of the lake. No Merlin.

I'm a castor. Words- a sword of burden.

02/07/2021

XXXV.

And what do I have that is own by you?
A heartbeat- the tick of our mortal hours-
The tell-tale pulse deafening all we do.

That's a music pounding against eardrums-
An ocean captured in seashells- towers
Clicking from gears- haunting notes in seer-hums.

You are my Virgil, my faith, my sigil,
A felt of shadow deep in the darkness-
The voice overpowering fate's vigil.

To part from you is to forsake my soul-
To abandon what was forged in success:
The element of stars- our true parole.

We are the sun-life, the revelation,
Revolution after revolution.

XXXVI.

Here stands my hope, buried but resurfaced.

You treaded on it once. The contempt I felt.

What suffering could undo a purpose?

To be imprisoned within skin and bone;

The eternal trapped in a decayed self?

The greatest hell would be to call it home.

No one is a martyr, a unique cause.

We are all a part of a religion-

A belief that life exists despite flaw.

Be it anarchy or a designed test,

To be conscious precedes a decision-

An essence before breath can then oppress.

I refuse to sink into nothingness.

That's a free condemn not from emptiness.

02/09/2021

XXXVII.

The snickers when you rattle your own chains-
The notion that there's an ownership to them,
A right to enslave, trademark those in pain-

Forgets that slavery evolves with time.
Be it house or field. Be lining a hem
Or mining a gem. Be law or a crime.

The oppression may ease- may be welcomed
By those conditioned and those worked weary-
It still feeds the machine the weak and numb.

Children raised in peace will play games of war-
That doesn't mean there's no faith for a theory,
Spiritus Mundi - for us to explore

And to drown in the all, the history,
The collective steam of humanity.

XXXVIII.

Weary with the world I laid in your bed-
A funeral repose- but you were gone,
Fashioned for a date with the truly dead.

An old soul living in a modern world-
That's what I told myself and everyone-
Why suffer to see all I love unfurled?

I sought you out, harvested but unravished,
Wanting all the pleasure, not the pain-
A pilgrimage to pray with the vanished.

I arrived too early- maybe too late.
I waited, closed my eyes, made my limbs lame
But my thoughts pointed out that wasn't my fate.

When we meet, I will kiss you, Death, my way.
I will be the one to take breath away.

02/10/2021

XXXIX. From Orpheus: to Charon I

The dance of Danace- the cadence of oars-
Plunging deeper in waters of because-
I'll give you an oath until we reach shore.

A Words-worth of willow swaying about-
Memories of what is and never was -
Shadowing the direction of the boat.

My words are yours, use them as you need them
Like living men translating withered scrolls
And dictate meaning among the condemn.

You beat and beat against the waves of hands, -
Those who weigh too heavy to swim with soul-
All because you had no voice to command?

Paddle away but pity the suicides-
Those of strength, tired by rising tides.

XXXIX: From Orpheus: to Charon II

Years I lingered on the shore, breathed that air.
To lose everything I once held so dear.
That cost was a cross too heavy to bear.

Shattered souls came to drown, came to ponder.
Some slipped carelessly, trembling with fear
And others dived in to answer wonders.

The river and its currents welcomed them-
The brave sank, the desperate learned to swim-
The depths are endless, full of treasured gems.

Seldom few swam their way back to the shore.
None ever crossed. And now I sing this hymn,
You'll guide me to meet destiny once more.

Believe me, Death, I would not die for you.
Honesty- that's a strength mankind once knew.

IV.

As the leaves turn in color, you and me,
Hand in hand, all together, walk the woods,
Darkened in the middle of this journey.

Abandon all love who will enter here.
A sign read where a paved pathway once stood
And now stretches out in ruined despair.

We could have lingered there or took the path.
Instead, we made our own way through the trees,
A dangerous game lovers play with wrath-

The wrath of altering what is called fate.
The beast of time in prowl, scent in the breeze,
We can return to the trail or head straight.

We will plunge deeper into this affair-
Exit pursued by the passion we bear.

02/11/2021

IVI.

Don't pity the butterfly- their short life.

Feel for those pinned in prosperity's frame-

Markings brilliant, colors a vibrant-strife.

Monarchs count not the lives but the journey,

Fluttering against the wind, braving rain.

It's the miles flown- moments lived- the dream,

The dream to migrate toward paradise,

Not for them, but for those, yet to be born,

That gives them courage to keep flight precise.

Where is my sense for dawn's light in the dark?

A fearlessness to power through the storm,

Not to seek out shelter and then embark?

The worst you could be is to crystal this-

The nihilist safe in his chrysalis.

02/12/2021

IVII: Beast of Beauty

I.

Eros, the Cupid, the winged jester,

Felt an itch his arrows could only scratch.

Did it once- then let the desire festered.

A fever brewed with no remedy near.

Unlike Narcissus, Eros saw no match

When his beauty stared back in pool of tears.

Self-wounded he, who pierced the hearts of stone,

Built altars with the flings from his bow-string

And breathed virgin choirs of lonely moans.

He needed a Psyche. - But where was she?

He searched far. In the wind, he heard her sing

Tales of abandonment and jealousy.

That was when the gods of all that is vain

Commanded him to inspire her to love shame.

II.

He refused to aim- wound her like others.
"Pity makes us mortal." Father War said.
"Hunters do not take the prey as lovers."

"Psyche can only be tamed by a beast."
Mother Night laughed. "She'll sleep soon in dew's bed
If you do not shoot and she finds no priest."

Eros could feel the infection morph him.
He chose to be the monster in shadows,
The creature Olympus felt to be grim.

In the still night laid out like an abyss,
He roamed, staggering still from his arrow,
And found Psyche, blood dripping from her wrist.

He whisked her away- his wings feathered flight-
And nursed her to health, where there was no light.

III.

There- where only touch and voice could exist-
They lingered, confessing pain and pleasure;
How each of them felt a part was amiss.

To spend an eternity there, they would-
But the Fates found them, eager to sever-
And revealed to Olympus all they could.

The gods sent the dawn to peak upon them-
Cast light upon what Eros kept hidden.
Psyche rose first to find a beast of sin.

Her pulse quickened - Her lips quivered to speak -
As the sunlight reveal the forbidden-
And Eros awoke to tears on her cheek.

That's when the Belle of his soul spoke his name-
And healed the wound that had bound him in chains.

IV.

She loved him- though the gods left him a freak-

And he could never be without her near,

Although a mortal she was- yet unique.

Zeus found no comedy with the farce

And offered to change how Eros appeared

As long as he kept his time with her sparse.

Eros refused and left his bow unstrung;

Denied the gods their comedy and drama.

All he wanted was Psyche to stay young.

The cicada hiss from the bedded grass

Warned him to not challenge the panorama-

Yet he urged that she be him, him her glass.

And so, soul merged with love, and you with me-

Once the gods had realized what had to be.

02/13/2021

XLIII.

Never have I found God in cathedrals,

Felt myself vaulted or spiraled in faith,

So much to need maps of the cerebral.

To stand inside so much space, to be air-

A trick in losing self to be a wraith-

Can be admired with no need for prayer.

Yellow woods- a stone pathway, worn by moss,

The rasp of air whistling through dead elms,

A trickling stream - a childhood now lost.

The closest I come is with words and lines. -

It is with you- I find a divine realm-

A holiness not contained by designs.

To feel the soul without architecture

Draws one to speak of your love like scripture.

02/14/2021

XLIV: A Poet's Wake

I.

Eyes startled open from a dream of life,
I awoke in a salon, full of ghosts
Tattooed by ink and not fearful in sight.

I climbed out of bed, the pillowed casket,
To make sense of why the dead left their posts
And I found myself the soul unblanketed.

In this funeral, the spirits gathered,
An academy of poets I have known,
Intellect and their manners untattered.

Burns looked straight through me, nodded at Auden-
Followed by Merwin and Ashberry- his clones. -
As if I couldn't even be forgotten

'Cause what I have done couldn't be remembered
Like the pale sunlight in cold December.

II.

Then I took a brief survey of the room:
Blake hummed innocence. Plath sat all gloomy.
Eliot played the critic. Sam enjoy shrooms.

Dante and Donne had islands of their own.
Tagore, Sappho played rummy with Rumi.
Yeats droned on his mad love Gonne all alone.

Clare laughed. William couldn't find his words worthy.
Byron sulked. Keats sipped on a blood-clot wine.
Shelley read up on Marxist philosophy.

Poe and Thomas slept, too drunk for death's masque.
The Brownings locked in a kiss, full of sighs,
While Ginsberg and Hughes jazzed up a flask.

All came for Shake-speare, unmasked as De Vere,
Not to welcome me, their dead, as a peer.

III.

I fled to a dark room; door cracked to hear-
My sanctuary- a fain of the few.
In the shadow, I could feel some still near.

"Who are you?" Dickinson asked. "Nobody?"
I am Odysseus, a nobody too,
Sharpening the pencil for those that see.

"Oh, so clever to hide within the lines."
Whitman sneered. "The people want nakedness,
Not allusions, conceits, meter and rhymes."

Rilke shrugged, tired of the Calvary.
"A rose wilts with petals of openness;
Closed within itself, it learns of beauty."

I write to own meaning, myself alone,
Wishing time can find worth in what I owned.

IV.

I left that room- to find where I belonged:
Nowhere. - I snuck into the library
To study what I have done wrong in song.

There- a motley view- I found him hidden-
He, who words I breathe leaves my lungs icy,
So much that my soul dares to leave prison.

I had no right to stand in his presence-
The great bard with no peer in history.
No word of mine could match his elegance.

He peered back- knowing he wasn't invisible-
His purple robes stained, his name a story.
He then spoke, a truth miserable.

"Say my name and all you hear is violence.
The writing is all. The rest is silence."

V.

I let him be- though I wanted to stay.
I realized where I belonged: In the box
Where my body was laid in full display.

A few of the bards were too dead to care.
Most wondered why I held the muses' phlox-
For them a promise that a there is there:

I am not a poem. I'm a poet-
A sea you drown in to gasp complete depth,
Never to know the multitudes' moment.

Compare to all of you, I am nothing,
Though I feel when I have breathed my last breath,
You will find a volcano, a hot spring-

And when the future sifts through the ashes,
They'll find Pompeii, a view for the masses.

02/15/2021

XLV.

Neon skyline- a leap of faith, not fear-
In the drop, do you feel a fallen star-
Suspended in air - a chandelier?

A snowy road, slippy turn- a car crash-
Investigators can't find truth from afar.
Long wake, harsh trauma- earned insurance cash.

Lil Bo-Weep, the wolf-party will be over
While Ophelia picks up forget-me nots-
The prince drowns. Telemachus discovers.

Widowed: empty home- soul and bones alone.
Crystal-year shatters to pieces- knows plot-
never says goodbye or let it be known.

These are puzzle-words of what could have been;
A fate-web spun, tink from begin to end.

02/16/2021

XLVI. From Orpheus

I came to Delphi, center of the world,
Seeking out the holy rites of the mind
And see what the oracles could unfurled.

Lips stained, they slurred to speak what's understood
By a wine: summer's blood from a grape vine
Pruned by winter- one year sprout now brown wood.

Beware the awareness- petals in bloom-
The focus peers outward, not from within,
Clouded by the sly riddles and perfumes.

Set sail, you, Odysseus with ocean eyes
And forget Ithaca, all of your kin,
For the horizon of adventures' whys.

To forget myself, become someone new-
That would have been death to all I knew.

02/17/2021

XLVII: Orpheus

The stars claimed my lyre. They claimed my head.
Numb of body and soul, lyric and beat,
The songs flowed from lips imprecise and dead.

Living day to day- not for tomorrow-
How long could I go on with that deceit-
When suicide feels like a blessed sorrow?

That sorrow- that grief in losing a self,
A self-devoted to her, poetry-
All would return to what we once had felt.

That was a journey welcomed by Hades.
No need to look back or ahead- just see
Oneself in pieces like the Cyclades.

I could have dwelt in silence, calm and brave,
While the nightingales sang over my grave.

XLVIII.

The nepenthe they gave- a quick slumber-
Poison flowering white with fern-like leaves-
Murdered lightening to quiet thunder.

Who was I to question the oracles,
Although I knew they loved to pierce through greaves
Forcing one to kneel? - Faith in miracles!

Shatter the trust in armor- you'll stand cold,
Seeking a warmth from the cocktails they brewed
And have no need to have feelings of old.

Dull the trauma you have upon the world. -
The rivers, nymphs, stones trickling songs in you
Lose sense of the wonders, your boys and girls.

Be for the Lotus Eaters an audience.
I'm not nobody. - I am Orpheus.

XLIX.

High above the River Styx - the frozen wake,

I made my wanderings into the night,

Sure-footed on crackling ice-mistakes.

The echoes: the past that has come alive,

Haunts the present-steps to future delights.

I hummed over them a will to survive.

What did I hum? Songs of mortality:

Hour glass cracked- a falling sand caught the wind:

A flight-tumble into obscurity

And death, my clarity. That's when I knew

The haziness over all that's within-

The slow let go- was not a pursued brew.

The rattle of breath plays the rhythm-day,

This battle to. . . A rhyme and a cliche.

L.

Weep not because I am only passing-
Passing by the experience of this world-
And merging into the spirit's blessing.

Weep for yourself, the loss of my presence,
Because I am not gone- only unfurled
What is a man. Noise, dust, then quiescence.

Let the ache of your soul throb through the flesh;
Remind you that the matter's energy
Cannot be destroyed, render down to ash.

I am the breeze, the air in which you breathe.
If you believe that these are elegy,
Seek me out in the spirit of the sea.

In that expanse of time, search for my name,
A song bird Death cannot cage, cannot tame.

02/18/2021

LI.

Passion, not love, has no vision;
No foresight in how futures meet
Or an eventual division
Exhausting folly from the heat.

Speed on, you clown-servant named Speed.
Fling like a blind-folded Cupid.
Seek your treasure in pleasure need
Until you can see what's lucid.

Fault romance- the eyes dewed with lies
That cannot chance the unpleasant
Or know a truth when it's disguised-
A merchant flame in the present.

True love loves with all the senses
Sensing flaws without pretenses.

LII.

Too often my thoughts travel with missteps-
A fall. - A spiral descent of terrors. -
That my feet struggle for balance in treks.

Doubt festers belief that nothing is real:
All is a mirage, a house of mirrors-
Where purpose and passion have no appeal.

The evil genius shatters the ego. -
So, the story goes until I declare:
I think myself so because I think so.

The certain in blooms, thorns adorn the stem.
Spring-dew becomes frost in the winter air;
The fragile hardens to a frozen gem.

The world that's seen by finite I- the eye
Reflects the stillness for others to find

02/20/2021

LIII.

The living doesn't often choose their coffin

Or leave behind the design that they want.

Most desire to deny Death all that's rotten.

The weary few plan a dreary dew end

Sprouting truth like a terrible enfant-

Hushed by the wind of what is forbidden.

Wills dictate what is to happen in law,

Though rules have no value for those that rule

And is useless in ink that lawyers draw.

So, when I have buried myself in words,

Leave me be as a rhyme-muttering fool

Or think of me as a caged-beaten bird.

Speech remains free when truth is a censure,

Although I remain barred from adventure.

02/22/2021

LIV.

Never could I stand in line, be content-
Hand on my heart, a prayer on my lips
And be the child that God in heaven sent.

The boats rowing down on the old Ohio.
The locust buzz. The stillness of eclipse.
That was a religion I longed to know.

I walked home: second-hand shoes' souls worn thin-
The Cincinnati skyline in the clouds.
My thoughts dared to be elsewhere like a wind-

Swirling above skyscrapers, flights of birds-
A wish to be unique among the crowds;
Life not defined by Death but put in words-

Experience not remembered but always felt.
The place to be wasn't there- but in myself.

LV.

Concern yourself with greatness, you will fail.

To describe the impossible in verse,

You'll blow wind directly in front of sails.

Angle the boat and let nature set coarse.

Zig-zag away from dangers, the gods' curse.

Drown out the Sirens that drown in lust's force.

Life's two stories: the stranger on journey

Or the one burdened with the odyssey-

The details are yours. The harbor many.

Rough winds stir up moonlight tides to break ships.

Brace for them. Learn to beat against the sea.

Taste the salty tears pressed upon your lips.

The suffering to be creates the art,

Not the labor to reach back to the start.

02/23/2021

LVI.

For Meggie: while she gets a deserved nap.

How do I
        know that
                you love me
Without rhythm,
        free from a form?

A freedom in spirit-
        A spirit that longs to be. -
Not the spirit,
        caged from what it should be,
Singing for the art of flight,
                a choice of scene.

If anyone cares
        To ask me who are,
What it meant to know you.
I would tell them:
A great woman in history
        If history means anything
And gender of birth can be allowed to be
As well allowed
        to be altered
                Or ?unsettled?

Who was she?
Parallel in history?

Cleopatra:
a fatal distraction-
A *crooked* crown
straightened by a servant-
A civil war dressed
as a play of passion?

Elizabeth:
the lover of the married-
A virgin myth
with no plan for an heir-
A rose war dieback,
An end to a line?

Victoria:
the mother of a nation-
The sheltered child
Destined to rule by birth-
Defined a generation,
Virtue and vice?

A monarch?
No, a Queen unto Herself,
Who rescued those from death,
Nursed the wounded with life
And sacrifice energy
To fuel other souls.

My lover.
My reason to be in flesh.

LVII. From Dandelion Queen: Zitkala

Dandelion. - Dandy lion. -

A weed to mow that always grows.

A flower I worn in my hair

Placed there by your hand-

          then we kissed.

Dandelion- the lion tooth.-

No thorns to cut, yet I still bleed.

I held you tight against my kiss

And inhaled your breath

          into my lungs.

As a child, I played the lawn game,

Popping off mamma's baby heads;

A metaphor I leave for them.

For the part of you

          Still inside me:

You are my beauty, my common,

That taught me how to grow myself.

          2/24/2021

LVIII. From Orpheus: Dido

A fragment in verse,
>Virgil once detailed.
A hunting party,
>A thunderclap storm:
The summon of curse
>And scatter of trail.
Two lovers can be
>Caved in their desire
Refugees from rule
>And the noble scowls.
Her lips upon his,
>A quivering moan-
An omen for fools:
>The wolves deep in howls. -
The wanderer quiz:
>Stray now or be owned?
He came unconquered.
>She came to be loved.
A lust unsettled.
>A ship sailed off course.
A fate betrayal.
>A dagger drips blood.
Bloodlines now distance.
>Soul and flesh divorced.
A funeral pyre,
>A blaze on water-
A light now retired-
>Far from the harbor.

LIX.

Love: an ex machina in life-stories:

A love song: two hearts throbbing in cadence.

A shared whirlpool of fate: a shared journey.

Destiny rearranged- new quilt pattern,

Thread through the needle, thread through labyrinth:

A Bacchus tapestry in a tavern.

To think of you- bursts of insanity,

Where a spirit of solitude finds home

And catch the lightening of poetry.

Souls of matter must suspend energy,

Not be physical chemistry alone

Or shattered in pieces- science's tragedy.

If void is all that defines life, I can die,

Knowing I meant something real in your eyes.

LX.

Life can be a fable for the able-

Those that threw stones at the sky and made stars,

While grounded by high horses in the stable.

Nomad slingers aimed at Goliath foes,

The odds unfavored to be what they are

And let their wit take flight with skillful throws.

The lightning strike, the fall of the guard. -

Shepherds of the willow, crowned by slaughter,

The bootstrap mythology is theirs to reward.

I've gone crazy, tossing words in the well.

I cursed the reflection on the water

While the echoes found air, began to swell.

These poems l lift as paper lanterns-

Lights of prayers among heaven's patterns.

2/25/2021

LXI. MAGA

A clipped winged, caged bird with no song to sing;

To always be alive but numb of art;

That is not me. Wonder why the bars ring?

Those without feathered throat, feel the pulse of heart,

Beat themselves against the man-wrought constraints,

All in wish for sky, a need to depart.

Go on with the Sympathy of restraints;

Know the reasons why there are chirps for worms.

They're hungry to lash at others constraint.

Doomed to an eerie silence before storm-

A storm that will shatter the neat parlors,

The dumb birds know anger and what is warm.

See them now: red of head, blue in armor,

Give them freedom or they will die martyrs.

LXII.

Childhood: a memory that never fades.
The wind stirring over the blue-grass hills.
Oak-trees with a canopy of leaves shade.

The earth-scent, a harmony of nature.
A moon so bright, rivers flow through the rills.
The sense that you are not and are creature.

Chiggers lie in wait for those that lie,
Staring up at the misty clouds of stars,
And crickets strum a violin-alibi.

Flash- a blurred hologram of colored light-
Dark bodies winged for flight, not Bell-Jars,
Inspire brilliance to reach soulful heights.

That's a nostalgia for what never was;
A faith in possibility, not because.

02/26/2021

LXII.

The look- the need to let the body be-

And the pose of the head on a pillow:

The tilt upward toward the ?what? - haunts me.

The faces change. Names become forgotten.

Memory ripples calmly, then billows

Crashing upon thought's harbors once again.

And here you lie in repose, in a bed,

Where others souls have been weighed by last gasps.

Eyes focused on the beyond, on the ahead.

Your heart swoons a rhythm of Kentucky.

Your hand reaches out- distance exceeds grasp.

Your chest heaves a rattle frothing bloody.

For the slowing of pain-breath, morphine;

The life of me injecting death in thee.

02/27/2021

LXIII.

Plunge deep into history, you will know
Chaucer's shitty shepherds steered and sheared sheep,
Who wore wool fresh as a January snow.

No wolf came for the fold- no temptation.
Call him a hypocrite? - He kept his keep.
The illiterate flock found a salvation.

Friars, the drunken passions, loved the crowds,
So joyous in the pious show of faith,
And yet, human enough to be allowed-

Allowed to pilgrimage with the merchants:
Men and women of talent, trade, and filth,
So eager to seek advice from serpents.

Where would I be? Alone, anchored to night,
Dead to world, free to be: an anchorite.

02/28/2021

LXIV.

As dusk fell, the dust fell upon the world,
So did the wonder-rust of wanderlust-
The wilt trip into a guilt trap unfurled.

The old wives tell an old wise tale of trust,
A fate-quilt woven now burst at the seams
Being mended by needle-bones of thrush.

Feel the whirlwind of a world-end romance-
The stage curtain closing on the certain,
And tell me you can trace the stars of chance,

Dot out constellations, creation myths.
Flutter-by butterfly, free from burden,
Hatched from a chrysalis, a monolith.

I have no time dilation, just the trek;
Awaked nightmare for an insomniac.

LXV.

I died once to find torment in Heaven;
The gates flung open. Peter nowhere near
To deny admittance to those stained by sin.

A sign stood where the good book was once placed.
"Beware all is empty. Silence lives here;
Angels of praise have fallen blessed by grace."

Within the streets of gold, fencing of pearls,
Souls wandered, prayers forming on their lips.
No purpose found for them in this hushed world.

Blood thumped against my eardrum melody.
I composed lyrics, my own private scripts.
Those of faith escaped from eternity;

A suicide from the crossroad within.
What others called suffering felt like Passion.

03/02/2021

LXVI.

A journey back from the highway nature.
March sun melting away February snows,
Muddy trails exposing steps of creatures.

Forty winters of snow melted to now-
A detour from the pathway that I know-
Somehow the easiest I've ever known.

The stream to the river coos a babble.
Birds chirp song for the rituals of spring-
Notes individual, notes rabble.

The hum of traffic intervenes music
And interweaves with all the life that sings:
A symphony common and elusive-

The sound of awakening from a slumber;
Not the aftermath of trauma: thunder.

LXVII.

Behold the horsemen- the night mares in trot-
War, plague, famine, death free from the stable.
What sacred seal was broken? Left to rot?

The zealots cheer on a final judgement.
Not a single rider steers the fable-
A collection of souls caused the movement.

A New Jerusalem is not coming;
You, fools of faith, won't avoid by Rapture
The rumbling of what was worth building.

Babble you towers of triumph-trump.
If God exist, she will avoid capture
And allow the tumble toward a slump.

The hope for a future, not a dream nap,
Prepare us to rebuild the current map.

03/04/2021

LXVIII.

Madness: an impulse to draft verse in note;

These letters to a world that never reads-

Not because it can't but because it won't.

And why commit oneself to the constraints?

Howl at the moon like Bedlam escapees

And you will see how they call for restraints.

There is intelligence in seclusion;

To grow thoughts in a garden, pluck out weeds,

And to cultivate a wild illusion.

A conservatory of the posey-

A madhouse against the season of seeds-

That is the crafted art of poetry.

A winter of contempt frosts summer's grace.

Safe within these walls, beauty has its place.

03/05/2021

LXIX.

A bee who makes home in a lone flower;

A seed that grew from the crack in asphalt.

Two destinies sharing a fate-shower:

The hard rains, the fluff snow, the sleet of ice-

And the response to what causes a fault:

A split between hell or a paradise.

No change of heart when you know you who are:

The hive mind of a worker colony-

Or a common sprout, not a lion-tooth-star.

It is who you want to be, not who are-

That dream that can alter a reality.

My love, that is what we are from afar:

No American Scheme- an American Real:

The struggled to live, to think and to feel.

03/06/2021

LXX.

Death, leave the slow-whirl of darkness to me.

The grave under grey elms and yew-tree shade,

Your bed, tempts adventurers from the sea;

So much that they sink in despair and drown

Or plunge into the Sirens' serenade,

Believing that is where you can be found.

Winter howls in your absence from the earth.

Spring flourishes when you deny all is dead.

You are the mystery, the worth of birth.

Leave me the sweeping voices to possess-

And you can be a nymph or queen of dread.

My echoed thoughts, in the depths, will fluoresce

The forgotten unseen temples and rites:

Centuries, short of day but long in nights.

03/07/2021

LXXI.

To be read, not seen: an act of folly.

A destiny in court, a suit to dress

A beheading game - an ax and holly.

Knight of green, green of nature, green obscene,

You are the presence, the success transgressed,

The whistling winter of whispered ween.

I strike with evergreen. - In a year's time,

You will strike your blow- a test of virtue.

No kiss of fame. No girdle of sublime.

Pearl of poet, bobbed and weaved, wheeled the scene;

He severed head, tricked the plot of curfew.

I'm armed with the symbol, garland of green.

I'll breathe chapel prayers, hold my head still.

You'll crown me with a laurel wreath or kill.

LXXII.

Chem-trail over the lark nest. . . through the sun,

Split the world, the breast of nature in two:

The world of man and what can't be undone.

Pick-up parking, exhaust of silver smog,

Delphi fumes, headlight candlelight grew,

What truth is there to know among the fog -

Away from the modern spew of passion

And the industry to sell a killing?

See me- out of season, out of fashion-

An impure mongrel, a gypsy in Stu.

Cancel what you want, art will persist. - Sing!

Sex, you want? I won't stand naked for you.

Everyone can be a poem, a verse,

Not a poet obsessed with what was cursed.

03/09/2021

LXXIII.

A smile, closing the eyes from weeping tears, -
I offered my prayers to those above:
The birds of song with notes of atmosphere.

My hymns of common throat: silence. . . a dash. -
A broken heart of unreturned love.
Hope feathers soul. "Expect Icarus' crash."

I was told to be patient, to be kind,
Waiting for the time when truth would be mine.
A seagull, its grey wings spread for the sky-

That is what the world told me what I was,
But I will be raising from the ground to fly
Far from the pier, up in clouds of because.

Dismissed dreams of being a skyscraper;
I will remain high, nature's true flapper.

LXXXIV.

A green chapel, overgrown with cave-moss:
The shattered sheet of stones of a walkway.
The devil's snare in bloom foreign to frost.

There you will find the crevice in hillside,
The once pagan-worship, Saxon in lay,
Now purified by the Christ crucified.

Remove the stone slabs to find the coffin-
The restraints of the soul in poetry-
And read aloud what truly lies within.

Here lies a great bard, the world kept hidden,
The bright pearl-shine of a dark history.
Massey be his name, true words of Britain.

Beyond the shifted vowels and meaning,
The living can't deny the ghost, his being.

LXXXV: ode to Petty Page,

written while debating buying a Stink Skateboard for Lizzie.

I'll take the abuse, this turn of the cheek,

A slap of equalness, not for meekness

Or a public act to weakened the weak.

You pursued a role in the missionary.

Did it well? No, there was a wakefulness

While drowning in your soul's visionary.

I can feel that. That Brutus slap-for-realz.

You got your break from their reality,

Straight-jacket and all. No hallmark feels.

You preceded convention. I get that.

To survive trauma, you chose slavery.

That's where we part greatly. A simple fact.

No we. - You be you and I'll be me.

A skateboard- an icon bling- let it be.

03/10/2021

LXXXVI.

This church, a swaying in the incense-smoke,
The chemical of faith and ritual,
Earthy as the pagans among faced oaks.

Flashes of lightening, Gods of thunder,
A sacred grove- a leafing visual-
A mysticism to be shaded under.

Bog Virgin- Dripping blade of sacrifice-
Druid high priest: all Roman impressions.
Truth sprouted from the ground nourished by ice.

The madness of my body: a Hell.
This: a rebellion to pain-depression.
Born sick. - These are my prayers to be well;

The only Heaven found in written hymns.
Amend. A-men. A-women. . . To the end.

LXXXVII: Orpheus I.

Tore apart and barely breathing,

Left on the shore. Silence plenty.

All I wanted: notes of singing,

My song on the lips of many

And you to witness the passion;

The madness heard in a chorus.

Long after the flesh has ashen,

Long lives a memory for us-

The trauma of harsh chords in pitch,

The off-rhythm pulse of our thoughts.

Voodoo doll in need of a stitch;

Fate's pin and needles can't be bought.

I left my threads in the labyrinth;

Please follow them, my hyacinth.

03/11/2021

LXXXVIII: Orpheus II

Like Euripides in a cave,

Composing goat odes of torture,

Or De Vere lost in masquerade,

Spear-shaking the loss of nature,

I perform my part for the stage.

You say the lines, full of rhythm,

Storm through the stress, secret in sage.

Be an Oracle but rid phlegm,

The settled state of apathy,

And foretell future with taboo.

Here cast in bronze, patina green,

The hollowness inside rings true.

Deep within the cracks of the plinth,

Spring the renewal, hyacinth.

LXXXIX: Orpheus III

A careless footstep, a harsh sun,

A lover's pluck, a vase-cutie,

Murder of crows all murders one:

The bloom of hope, fragile beauty.

To survive, you must borrow down,

Fight the dirt that can suffocate

And sprout from a seed, then the ground-

Liberty! like a famous saint.

Grow- know the dangers, the seasons,

The jealous trample of foot. . .

To them you are life in treason.

You: smut-diamond among the soot.

Who else could you share stars-map with?

Just you and me, my hyacinth.

XC:

A type-rope act from genius to madness,
A marriage between subconscious and thought.
No net with shame below- that's not rashness.

That's skill, a set-art made from disorder.
I practiced falls, mastered them and then sought
These flights of fancy, visions of grandeur

Tremor, yes. Tumble? Death: she's my servant.
What does it mean to not breathe, down in love:
A romance bipolar in its currents?

I am always higher than the audience-
But caught between the earth and sky above.
An unnatural step of a consequence.

Paint the white canvas of a page with blood-
(That's what you think I'll do?) - or paint with mud.

03/12/2021

XCI:

New motto: I came, they saw, you conquered.

No one questions the quiet quarrel-

The rewrite of laws or spoils squandered.

That silence, absence of civil crisis,

Willingly crowns a Caesar with laurel.

What does the populace believe of this?

Thumb in: "Make him know that he is dying".

A death in love, a Sabina in drag,

A spurious spore that beds a lying?

Or a conspiracy before conquest:

An idle March springing out of a lag,

A contest with Hellenistic expanse?

Perhaps a late arrival to the rite,

A Cinna of bad verse, a head on pike.

03/13/2021

XCII: written after a dream of the past

There among the disheveled crabapples,
Wind-whipped on the white cliffs washed by the sea,
Chanting the chaplet of rosewood chapels,

I saw you- gathering pips for the fire.
A name would be whispered. Whose would that be?
Did those pips burn or explode with desire?

In the dark, the daisy day-eyes are enclosed.
Visions of Albion stalks all that's stem-
Planted in foreign soil, the decomposed.

In the sunlight, you become history-
A ghost contrasted with white- A not-for-them,
Whose hearts do not pulse an ancestry.

I live because you loved. - From love: a tree
Blossoming still throughout the centuries.

03/14/2021

XCIII:

Open up to me, my sweet Ophelia,
The Pink lily among the turf of red
Or drown among the drowsy gardenia.

The sunlight cast a silent silhouette.
The river reverbs the revere ahead.
The trees shade sober-sere but statuesque.

Can you forget, picking forget-me-nots?
Tales of fairy campion companion
Blooms, despite the wintry cold of thought.

A break from co-dependency with life,
Not a dance on the edge of a canyon,
That's a madness that weds the day with night.

The swell- the cloister bells among the clouds.
Hidden among nature, your heart beats it aloud.

XCIV:

You were told you were sweet; the heights were short.

Little did they know you would be the tree,

Not a fruit that a hungry kiss might court.

The wind swept you away. A tumble hard.

Bruised deep inside, you festered free to be.

Naked of flesh, there was nothing to guard.

Frost blighting hours came for all that flowers.

Trampled by foot, you were buried in hurt,

Safe from the seasons and fate's many showers.

The strength in sadness, the growth from the tears,

The patience: A sprout that rose from the dirt,

Then a harden bark unseen by the years.

Love of life, these blossoms are of myself-

Delicate they may be, all real and felt.

XCV:

Telemachus, you're learning my story. -
Not the man that deserted but loved you
So much that he swerved to fight in glory.

Far from battle, fighting from an afar:
That's the name I gave you to live in verse,
To navigate patterns throughout the stars.

Troy fell for a trick pony. We all do.
Mine is feigned madness: a reflecting pool,
Where I can see the world among the blue.

The motif that I want you to understand:
I escaped fate by wearing the herd's wool,
And struck the one-eyed shepherd as no man.

Be proud: I'm Odysseus of the sea-
A mortal that has mastered the gods' schemes.

03/15/2021

XCVI.

Silver moonlight moves silent on the sills,

Slants the shallow movement of the still steep-

And I exist with some sparkling skills.

The nude, the profane, the untouchable:

A phantom fantom, a deep six in sleep-

A flight of dream that is undeniable.

You think I'm fluttering among the stars:

A caterpillar cocoon-butterfly,

A metamorphosis to be what you are?

A Kafka insect. - A flamer of flights. -

A bee-thing.- That's what you must see so high.

In day I'm dull because I'm one with night.

You can't start fire when inside is the spark.

So what if I am lightning in the dark.

03/16/2021

XCVII: Orpheus

A white room, barred away from song:

A cactus windowed from the snow,

Dying of thirst, away from sun.

A metaphor of youth I know.

Of all you can speak about me,

Please tell them that I went to hell.

No suffering there. Not my scene

And not much beauty in the tell.

The tragedy came in return.

Lyre laid to rest. Lifeless hymns.

Severed body. A pain that burns.

Thoughts violent. A cry of violins.

Tremble? Fear living in these times?

My words now dance on the fault-lines.

XCVIII: Saint Patrick's Day

A celebration of obscene:

A river dyed: a spring symbol,

A pinch of green, a drunken scene,

A history not assembled.

The Slainte asleep in silence:

Indentured servants stand solemn,

Not as slaves, violins of violence,

Or natives given blood omens.

The know nothing, the sneering sting,

Snuffs the secret flame of success

And gives us leprechauns that sing

Folkish foolery of excess.

That is the trap, the gold rainbow,

The myth that hides the trauma-woe.

XCIX.

A volcano- a delay in reaction,
The constant pull and romance with chaos-
The infernal stirring of emotion.

A love that is present in viewpoints,
Dismissed as nature's cauldron of pathos
Until fury melts what passion anoints.

And when the lava consumes and then cools,
Future generations will settle again,
Confident that they'll not burn like those fools,

Preserved by the hollowness of their lives.
They will not heed the warning smoke or singe;
To die, baptized by fire and harden rife.

Sleeping. . . Inactive from what can be seen,
Behold the danger that changes a scene.

03/17/2021

C: Indian Crossings

A skipping stone: a skillful throw of chance.

The past has not pass if it still ripples

Across the present's surfaced circumstance.

Fingerprints in the water in the stream:

Wind-blown patterns, whirlpools of the simple-

Individual currents made regime.

Orbs of sunlight unseen by passer-bys

Sparkle like Seraphim of forever

Visible to those with mystic-set eyes.

As the season scenery changes now,

A promise of never becomes severed.

In the rebirth, haikus sprout nature's vows.

How little life changes from day to day! -

Yet, is in a constant cycle and age.

03/18/2021

CII: Orpheus

Heroes are remembered in the lives saved

As long as those that live offer up praise.

Villains, empowered by those in the grave,

Need no voice to keep memories ablaze.

So, the villain I'll be to all that's wrong

And heroic toward the just oppressed.

My voice is straggled, broken in these songs:

They are for you to sing and seek success.

As free as you are, my children of verse,

You need to be released from the shackles,

Tethering you to the crags as a curse.

I can hear the fire that sparks and crackles.

Tied to the mast while sailors were bee-waxed,

I have shared your experience unrelaxed.

CIII: on Shaxberd

The swing and hum, the dance of pendulum. -
Violins voiced violets violent.
Mermaids marooned in myth attended him,

Whose footprints of words cast no muddy tracks
Treading toward the taverns of talent
Or reverberated the reverend step-facts.

A Fisher's Folly: a net that ensnares,
Traps the trout, trained them to trickled out Wit
And dissolves as if it never was there.

Who survives the plunge? Only the Spear-man-
Whose presence with water has no writ,
No Richard in rebels' recital-stand.

Like an axe bee-waxed from honey-tree chop,
Please see the splinters in history's prop.

03/19/2021

CIV: Hades and the Cartesian Court

The demons of reason creep from deep sleep,

Unseen in the dreams windswept by the sea,

To gnaw hope raw, keeping solace in weeps.

Wail the ailments well dry in moments' depths.

Comfort comes from ports computing a scene-

A percept in the concept of our breaths.

Shatter the shards, fragments of crystal thoughts-

I write therefore I am written. . . Am art,

A book bound, too black market to be bought.

I am not death. Only a collector-

A poetic Ryuk - a haiku heart -

The jester of gestures- the law-trickster.

Unyielding to the oaths of existence,

Deadling, you'll know from hell what fiction is.

03/20/2021

www.ingramcontent.com/pod-product-compliance
Lightning Source LLC
Chambersburg PA
CBHW051227160726
47994CB00002B/787